Holy Spirit My Partner for All Round Success

Kwadwo Boateng Bempah

Published by Dr. Kwadwo Bempah, 2024.

While every precaution has been taken in the preparation of this book, the publisher assumes no responsibility for errors or omissions, or for damages resulting from the use of the information contained herein.

HOLY SPIRIT MY PARTNER FOR ALL ROUND SUCCESS

First edition. December 2, 2024.

Copyright © 2024 Kwadwo Boateng Bempah.

ISBN: 979-8230345817

Written by Kwadwo Boateng Bempah.

Also by Kwadwo Boateng Bempah

Engaging The Law Of Seedtime And Harvest for Abundant Overflow
God of Miracles
Holy Spirit My Partner for All Round Success
Jesus The Great Physician: He is the master surgeon who heals all manner of sicknesses and diseases

Table of Contents

Introduction 1
Chapter 1 3
THE SUCCESSFUL CHURCH (BODY OF CHRIST) 4
Chapter 2 8
Who is the holy spirit? 9
Chapter 3 13
The Oil Of Influence 14
Chapter 4 17
The Holy Spirit Empowers You With Boldness 18
Chapter 5 22
The Seven Spirits Of God 23
Chapter 6 Manifestations Of The Spirit 29
SPEAKING IN TONGUES (As evidence of the baptism of the Holy Spirit) 42
Chapter 8 47
The Gifts Of The Holy Spirit 48
Chapter 9 57
The Fruits Of The Spirit 58
Chapter 10 59
The Anointing 60
Chapter 11 66
How To Catch The Anointing 67
Chapter 12 72
How To Activate The Power of The Holy Spirit 73
AMAZING TESTIMONIES 77

Holy Spirit
My Partner for All Round Success

Kwadwo Boateng Bempah

Introduction

••••

THE HOLY SPIRIT, MY partner for all round success, is the title of this book in your hands. We live in a world ruled by spirits. Most are evil spirits tormenting and destroying destinies. The ordinary person will find it difficult to succeed without the backing of a greater spiritual power. In Christ Jesus, we receive the Holy Ghost to dwell in us. He is the reason for our success in everything from ministry to personal living. When He comes into your life He brings all round success. That means total or complete success, nothing missing, nothing broken, nothing lacking.

He will turn every failure into a success. All you need, is to seek His presence all the days your life.

"And all Judah rejoiced at the oath: for they had sworn with all their heart, and sought him with their whole desire; and he was found of them: and the Lord gave them rest round about." (2 Chronicles 15:15)

We are told in the above scripture that when Judah decided to seek, desire, pursue and serve God with all their heart, He gave them all round (total) rest. He gave them peace and victory. Who gave them rest? The Lord.

2 Corinthians 3:17 tells us *"Now the Lord is that Spirit: and where the Spirit of the Lord is, there is liberty."* Notice: "...Now 'the Lord is that Spirit'..." This means the Spirit of the Lord is the one that gave them rest roundabout. It was total victory. Looking at Acts 10:38, we see *"How God anointed Jesus of Nazareth with the Holy Ghost and with power: who went about doing good, and*

healing all that were oppressed of the devil; for God was with him."

Here scripture says, Jesus was anointed with the Holy Ghost and power and He went about "...healing all..." This suggests that through the Holy Ghost, Jesus gave the people total freedom. It now makes it clear that to enjoy total freedom and success in every area of your life, you need the Holy Spirit. This is the reason I am writing this book, to help you discover the vital role the Holy Spirit plays in our lives and how He gives us success. **Note:** (Both Holy Spirit and Holy Ghost refer to the same Personality). I pray that before you finish reading this book you will be so anointed for all round success.

Chapter 1

THE SUCCESSFUL CHURCH (BODY OF CHRIST)

he Holy Spirit is the reason behind the success of the universal church and so is the individual's success also connected to Him. This end time church is a church of champions and giants.

"And it shall come to pass in the last days, that the mountain of the Lord's house shall be established in the top of the mountains, and shall be exalted above the hills; and all nations shall flow unto it." (Isaiah 2:2)

This scripture introduces the end time church of which we are all a part. It is a church ordained for beauty, authority and dominion. It is a solution bearing church. It is the modern day Noah's ark. It is a church that wipes away tears, refines and decorates destinies. It is a church made up of kings and priests, not nonentities (Rev 5:10). It is made up of a people of influence, but our influence depends on how well we know and walk with the Holy Spirit.

Walk in the Spirit

Feelings are the voice of the flesh. If you are walking by feelings, you are being dominated by the flesh. But the Bible tells us to crucify the flesh.

If the flesh is crucified, the voice of the flesh is also to be crucified. You cannot walk by feelings and be a successful Christian; for, if you are walking by feelings, then your flesh, and not your spirit, is dominating you. And you cannot walk by reason and be a successful Christian either, because reason is the voice of your mind.

HOLY SPIRIT MY PARTNER FOR ALL ROUND SUCCESS

However, you can walk by faith and be a successful Christian, because faith is of the Spirit. Walking by faith is letting your spirit man dominate you. We need to learn how to put the 'Greater One' who indwells us and who has infilled us to work for us. When we do, we will have no need to walk by sight, to look at circumstances, or to be ruled by our feelings.

We can rise above our physical limitations and natural circumstances and enter into the realm of the supernatural through the power of the Holy Spirit! That is real success. The spirit realm always dominates the physical realm, so the more spiritual you are, the more successful you become. The Holy Spirit makes us successful by making us influential. What is influence? It is simply, power to affect persons or events. The power of the Holy Spirit gives you success by helping you to influence your generation. He is the engine behind great achievement. The Holy Spirit makes us a success and through us, others are also made successful. He opens the truth of God's word (John 8:32) to us which brings us freedom from bondage and grants us access to the good life in Christ. We are standing high with Jesus and we bring that power to raise others to stand with us in our exalted position. The Holy Ghost in us transforms ordinary men into kings and priests.

We affect our environment with positivity. Let us look at the amazing truth these scriptures bring to us. ***"Ye are the light of the world..."*** Matt 5:14 ***"Ye are the salt of the earth..."*** Matt 5:13

This means you matter to this generation by divine selection. We are carriers of God's power. You are not born to live an ordinary life but rather, an extraordinary one in Christ Jesus. You are a city set on a hill that cannot be hidden. You have a golden destiny. As gold is influential in every part of the world, so are you!

[1] Then the angel who had been talking with me woke me, as though I had been asleep. [2] "What do you see now?" he asked. I answered,

"I see a gold lampstand holding seven lamps, and at the top there is a reservoir for the olive oil that feeds the lamps, flowing into them through seven tubes. (Zechariah 4:1-2 TLB)

What gives us such success and influence?

[6] Then he said, "This is God's message to Zerubbabel: 'Not by might, nor by power, but by my Spirit, says the Lord Almighty-you will succeed because of my Spirit, though you are few and weak.'(Zechariah 4:6 TLB)

Understand that for any believer to be successful and influential, it takes the Holy Spirit. So when a believer is filled with the spirit and consistently walks in the spirit, his success and influence would be felt by both people and the environment around him. That is God's plan for you. God wants you to become so successful and influential in ministry, business, academics, finance and in all areas that matter in life. People will now follow you to church to find out your secret. Many will chase you to know where your success emanates from.

Your personal influence will lead to church growth. You will become the fulfilment of; *"Thus saith the Lord of hosts; In those days it shall come to pass, that ten men shall take hold out of all languages of the nations, even shall take hold of the skirt of him that is a Jew, saying, We will go with you: for we have heard that God is with you." (Zechariah 8:23)*

Your life will not make meaning until you are filled with the Holy Spirit (oil of influence).

"And Jesus returned in the power of the Spirit into Galilee: and there

went out a fame of him through all the region round about." (Luke 4:14)

You will be successful and influential because you are having the overflow of the oil of the Holy Ghost.

How can I walk in the overflow of the spirit to succeed and influence my generation?

You must be filled with the Spirit (Eph 5:18). Being filled with the Spirit is where the success of the believer begins. *"...**Not by might or power but**

***by the spirit.**"*(Zechariah 4:6).

Chapter 2

Who is the holy spirit?

? is a question every believer must ask and get the right answer from scriptures. ◊is because the Holy Ghost is too important for the Christian, and we cannot be ignorant of His being and nature.

In answering the question of who the Holy Spirit is, many have thought; He is a wind, oil, fire, cloud or even water. Some also think he is tongues

or a shaking. As much as these symbols and experiences may relate to His nature and character, He is more than any of these.

THE HOLY SPIRIT IS A PERSON

Jesus refers to the Holy Spirit as a Person in John 14:16: *"... I will pray the Father, and he [the Father] shall give you another Comforter, that*

HE [the Comforter, the Holy Spirit] may abide with you for ever."

◊e Holy Spirit is a Person. In other words, when we receive the Holy Spirit, we receive Him, the third Person of the God-head, not an "it."

Jesus said; "... that HE may abide with you for ever" (John 14:16).

◊e Holy Spirit is the third person of the God-head. He is God. He is the power of God. He is the power behind healing, miracles, signs and wonders. He is God's promise to you.

5 For John truly baptized with water; but YE SHALL BE BAPTIZED

WITH THE HOLY GHOST not many days hence...8 But ye shall receive power, AFTER THAT THE HOLY GHOST IS COME UPON

YOU: and ye shall be witnesses unto me both in Jerusalem, and in all Judea, and in Samaria, and unto the uttermost part of the earth. (Acts 1:5,8)

32 ◊is Jesus hath God raised up, whereof we all are witnesses. 33 ◊erefore being by the right hand of God exalted, and having received of the Father THE PROMISE of the Holy Ghost, he hath shed forth this, which ye now see and hear. (Acts 2:32,33)

Note that in Acts 1:5 and 8, Jesus spoke of the promise of the Holy Ghost to the Church — the Body of Christ. He said, *"... ye shall be baptized*

with the Holy Ghost..." (Acts 1:5). And in Acts chapter 2, we see the fulfillment of that promise. Then in Acts 2:38 and 39, Peter told the

people that the promise of the Holy Spirit was given to as many as believed. *38 Then Peter said unto them, Repent, and be baptized every one of you*

in the name of Jesus Christ for the remission of sins, and ye shall receive

THE GIFT OF THE HOLY GHOST. 39 For THE PROMISE is *unto you, and to your children, and to all that are afar off, even AS MANY as the Lord our God shall call (Acts 2:38,39).* In other words, those who are

born again. The Holy Spirit is God's gift He promised mankind (those who believe in Jesus). He is exactly like Jesus. Before Jesus left the earth He said,"I will pray the Father and He shall give you another comforter". In the Greek language, that is 'Allos Parakletos', meaning "another one that is

exactly like me, to go along with you."

"And I will pray the Father, and he shall give you another Comforter, that he may abide with you for ever;" (*John 14:16*)

Jesus was saying, the Father will send to you another one exactly like me, called to go alongside you. The Holy Spirit therefore looks like Jesus;

He talks like Jesus, He loves like Jesus, He helps like Jesus and works like Jesus. This means whatever Jesus would do for you if He were here

physically, the Holy Spirit is here doing exactly the same for us, so cheer up. Reading from the Amplified Bible, it becomes clearer what the comforter does for us in His ministry to the saints.

"And I will ask the Father, and He will give you another Comforter (Counselor, Helper, Intercessor, Advocate, Strengthener, and

HOLY SPIRIT MY PARTNER FOR ALL ROUND SUCCESS

Standby), that He may remain with you forever-" (John 14:16 AMP)

The Holy Spirit is the one who counsels (advises) us to make right decisions. He helps us to do whatever we are called to do. He acts as an intercessor, who backs us up in prayers. He acts as an advocate to defend and speak on our behalf. Moreso, acting as our strengthener, he gives us strength to run the race of life without fainting. Finally, as our standby, he supplies us power to keep going when we get tired and lose energy.

The Holy Spirit is the treasure in our earthen vessels. He makes us strong and unbeatable even in the face of harsh, difficult circumstances and heart-breaking challenges.

"But we have this treasure in earthen vessels, that the excellency of the power may be of God, and not of us. We are troubled on every side, yet not distressed; we are perplexed, but not in despair; Persecuted, but not forsaken; cast down, but not destroyed;"
(2 Corinthians 4:7-9)

The Holy Spirit is the 'Greater One' who lives in us.

Smith Wigglesworth, a man of God who was used mightily by the Lord to preach faith and perform miracles of healings, said in his book - EVER INCREASING FAITH, "I am a thousand times bigger on the inside than I am on the outside." Here, this great man of faith was commenting on the scripture *"...greater is he that is in you, than he that is in the world" (1 John 4:4).*

Papa Hagin, reading this from Wigglesworth also said, "I began to see it then. With this enlightened understanding, I felt Wigglesworth should have said, "I am a million times bigger on the inside." That still would not have done it justice because God is infinitely bigger than we can

think or imagine. Someone asked Wigglesworth, "What is your secret to the great place of
spirituality you have attained?" His answer was, "All I ever did was to remember that greater is He who is in me than he who is in the world."

I sincerely think we all must have this word-based mentality about the
Holy Spirit. He is greater than any power and His presence within us makes us greater than any challenge. This means, we are a success
everywhere and in all things, with Him in us. Glory to God! This is exciting! Ladies and gentlemen, my fellow believers, this is why we need the Holy Spirit more than ever before in our life's pursuit. Without Him life will be frustrating and humiliating. But with Him, it is possibility all the way. Get to know Him and you will enjoy life. Since I have known Him, life has been from glory to glory and success to success.

Chapter 3

The Oil Of Influence

Oil is a type of the Holy Spirit. There is a great need for the oil of influence. Christianity without the Holy Ghost will be powerless and colorless. He is the one that gives us shape and form. (Gen. 1:2)

He is the sweetest companion anyone can ever have. The Holy Ghost was purposely given among other things to make us influential. (Acts 10:38)

-He is given to us to impact our world. (Acts 1:8)
-He is given to us to guide us into truth. (John 16:13 14). He reveals Jesus to us. -He is given to us to comfort our world. (John 16:7) -He is given to us to heal our world. (Rom. 8:11) -He is given to us to teach (inform) us. (John 14:26) He informs us to transform us with heavenly information. The difference between failure and success is information. He is the

communicator of divine secrets that make us stars (1 Cor. 2:10). He connects us to heavenly wisdom that makes us unbeatable in the race of life.

We need Him;

- **To fulfil destiny.**

Every believer ought to be filled with the oil of influence so that God's purpose for your life can be fulfilled. Jesus told us that it is impossible

to fulfil our golden destiny without the oil of influence. (Zech 4:1-6)

Jesus' ministry remained unfulfilled until the Holy Ghost descended on Him to open up His destiny (Luke 4:1&18).

- **To silence the opposition.**

All life's battles are spiritual. To every destiny there is an opposition (John 10:10). The devil dreads our success and impact. So he constantly opposes us to make us failures. But with the Holy Spirit we travail to prevail.

HOLY SPIRIT MY PARTNER FOR ALL ROUND SUCCESS

So shall they fear the name of the Lord from the west, and his glory from the rising of the sun. When the enemy shall come in like a flood, the Spirit of the Lord shall lift up a standard against him. (Isaiah 59:19)

Here are very recent testimonies to buttress this scripture;

A lady was kidnapped by ritual killers and as they pulled her bag from her hands in the midst of others kidnapped and tied, the things in her bag fell down. Among them was a church flyer(poster) with the picture of her pastor (Bishop Oyedepo). When the flyer fell down, the picture began to speak in tongues and all 15 kidnappers fell 'under power' completely immobilised. The lady got up and released the others and they all escaped. In another testimony, a lady was searching for an apartment with her little son and came across a house being rented. She entered to make enquiries

only to find herself in the midst of ritual killers. In the room were corpses of people who had been killed with blood flowing all around. The killers told her she would not be leaving as they were going to kill her. This woman, a born again child of God immediately removed a bottle of

anointing oil from her bag and smashed it on the floor. It caught fire as she and her son shouted "Holy Ghost fire!". The killers now said "we have kidnapped the wrong person, open the door for her to go". As she turned to open the door, it refused to open so she took her mantle (an anointed

material from her pastor) and struck the door with it and it opened immediately and she was able to escape with her son. Glory to God.

This is the work of the Holy Ghost, make Him your partner today and you will escape all the attacks of the enemy. He is the limit lifter and

breaker (Luke 4:14, Isaiah 10:27). Jesus told us we will do greater works after He is gone according to John 14:12, because of the Holy Spirit.

- **To fill us with the full load of heaven's resources.**

"And to know the love of Christ, which passeth knowledge, that ye might be filled with all the fullness of God." (Ephesians 3:19).

In Isaiah 11:1-3, we are told Jesus had all that He needed to fulfil His ministry through the Spirit. The Holy Spirit makes it possible to receive the full load of God. This is why Jesus told them to wait and receive the full package before they set off (Act 1:4).

- **To give us raw power to break all limitations.**

"And, behold, I send the promise of my Father upon you: but tarry ye in the city of Jerusalem, until ye be endued with power from on high" (Luke 24:49)

HOW DO I ENGAGE THE MINISTRY OF THE OIL OF INFLUENCE?

- **Pray and ask for it.**

"If ye then, being evil, know how to give good gifts unto your children: how much more shall your heavenly Father give the Holy Spirit to them that ask him?" (Luke 11:13)

- **Exercise yourself frequently in speaking of tongues.**

(Jude 1:20) *"I thank my God, I speak with tongues more than ye all:"* (1 Corinthians 14:18)

- **Sing spiritual songs:**

"And be not drunk with wine, wherein is excess; but be filled with the Spirit; Speaking to yourselves in psalms and hymns and spiritual songs, singing and making melody in your heart to the Lord;" (Ephesians 5:18-19)

Chapter 4

The Holy Spirit Empowers You With Boldness

Boldness is one of the characteristics of the Holy Spirit and He ministers it to us when we receive Him.

"And when they had prayed, the place was shaken where they were as- sembled together; and they were all filled with the Holy Ghost, and they spake the word of God with boldness." (Acts 4:31)

In response to their prayer to God for deliverance from threats, God responded by filling them with boldness from the Holy Ghost. All we are saying is that many things are threatening us in life and the boldness of the Holy Spirit is the answer.

Most battles of life are lost on the grounds of fear. Without boldness, destiny cannot deliver. In the absence of boldness, plans and purposes suffer miscarriage. Boldness is the trademark of all winners. It takes boldness to attempt and accomplish great things for God. When you receive Him, you have received inner boldness to confront all threats and issues of life. ◊at is influence. Note: ◊e boldness here (Acts 4:31) is from the Greek word, "parrhesia" meaning;

- To speak openly, frankly.
- To speak with fearless confidence/ cheerful courage.
- Bluntness/publicity, that is without reservation. All outspokenness. Make bold declarations such as, "the devil is a liar!" "I cannot be poor."

"Devil you are too small. I'm above all your threats!"

Why did He give boldness in response?

To confront the spirit of fear that puts men and women in bondage.

Forasmuch then as the children are partakers of flesh and blood, he also himself likewise took part of the same; that through death he might destroy him that had the power of death, that is, the devil; And deliver them who through fear of death were all their lifetime subject to bondage. (Hebrews 2:14-15)

Now with this boldness you confront all negative issues of life. A righteous person has boldness in his spirit. *The wicked flee when no man pursueth: but the righteous are bold as a lion. (Proverbs 28:1)*

As a result of this boldness the believers spake (spoke) the word (Acts 4:1). The word "spake" used here is from the Greek word *"laleo"*-it means to talk, speak and declare. Note that this is a bit different from preaching even though it is implied.

The word for preaching in the Greek is *"kerusso"* (Matt 4:23), but here he uses *"laleo"* meaning, to utter a voice or sound or to use words in order to declare or speak. What he is saying is that with this boldness they spake (laleo) to;

• Cast out demons and their activities.

"And they were all amazed, and spake among themselves, saying, What a word is this! For with authority and power he commandeth the unclean spirits, and they come out." (Luke 4:36)

• Anytime you are confronted with any demonic interference just speak in tongues and speak with Holy Ghost boldness. The authority came

after Jesus returned in the power of the Holy Ghost

"And Jesus returned in the power of the Spirit into Galilee: and there went out a fame of him through all the region round about." (Luke 4:14)

The power of the Holy Ghost is "dunamis" in Greek. Meaning the following;

• Inherent power (power residing in a thing).
• Power for performing miracles.
• Power and influence that belongs to riches and wealth.
• Power and resources arising from numbers.
• Power resting upon armies and forces.
• The authority of a spiritual potentate (power superior to man) This simply means you must speak with boldness knowing you have

authority.
- Speak as a person of influence who is rich and wealthy.
- Speak with the boldness of a man who has the backing of multitudes
(masses).
- Speak with the boldness of a man having the backing of a great military force.

Note that this is the only way we can win the battles of life.
- To heal sicknesses and diseases when they show up.

"When Jesus saw that the people came running together, he rebuked the foul spirit, saying unto him, You dumb and deaf spirit, I charge thee,
come out of him, and enter no more into him. And the spirit cried, and rent him sore, and came out of him: and he was as one dead; in somuch that many said, He is dead." (Mark 9:25-26)
- To command miracles, signs and wonders.

"Long time therefore abode they speaking boldly in the Lord, which gave testimony unto the word of his grace, and granted signs and wonders to
be done by their hands." (Acts 14:3)
- Against fear of failure, bad dreams, accident, miscarriages, premature death, and negative prophecies.

"Let your conversation be without covetousness; and be content with such things as ye have: for he hath said, I will never leave thee, nor forsake thee. So that we may boldly say, The Lord is my helper, and I will not fear what man shall do unto me." (Hebrews 13:5-6)

Note that Jesus displayed boldness in all circumstances even against natural elements. *"And he arose, and rebuked the wind, and said unto*
the sea, Peace, be still. And the wind ceased, and there was a great calm. And he said unto them, Why are ye so fearful? how is it that ye have no faith?" (Mark 4:39-40)

HOLY SPIRIT MY PARTNER FOR ALL ROUND SUCCESS

We must act like our master. You are not to be threatened by anything because you have inner power from the Holy Spirit. You must walk in the liberty of the Holy Spirit. *"Now the Lord is that Spirit: and where the Spirit of the Lord is, there is liberty." (2 Corinthians 3:17)*

When you have the Father of all spirits dwelling in you by the Holy Spirit, then you are above all negative spirits of fear, sickness, depression, poverty, failure and the fear of death. *"Furthermore we have had fathers of our flesh which corrected us, and we gave them reverence: shall we not much rather be in subjection unto the Father of spirits, and live?"*

(Hebrews 12:9)

All spirits are subject to you when the Father of all spirits dwells in you by the Holy Ghost. ✧is is where our confidence and boldness comes from. ✧is makes us influential with the ability to effect every type of change. You do not cry when faced with challenges; you relax and declare a change with boldness! *"...the righteous are as bold as a lion" (Proverbs 28:1)*

Chapter 5

The Seven Spirits Of God

e Holy Spirit was given to make us successful. ⬧us Jesus said tarry till you are filled before you attempt anything if you do not want to fail
(Luke 24:49, Act 1:4, Zech 4:6).

When you receive the baptism of the Holy Spirit, know that it is not a onetime experience, recognize that a divine personality has come to live in you. A heavenly being has come to take residence in you.

"Even the Spirit of truth; whom the world cannot receive, because it seeth him not, neither knoweth him: but ye know him; for he dwelleth with you, and shall be in you." (John 14:17)

All you need is to be conscious of his indwelling presence and allow Him to do His work in you. You will succeed easily. Success is beautiful! ⬧at
is why people celebrate success. He (⬧e Holy Spirit) influences you to succeed.

How does He carry out that ministry?

Every child of God is a child of destiny (Rom. 8:28-30), but not all destinies get fulfilled. You need to be empowered to fulfil destiny. Jesus told the apostles that when they receive Him, they will succeed in winning souls. Soul winning is the greatest business on earth; so get on it and help many to fall in love with Jesus!

He comes as the seven Spirits of God and can turn every one into a success. Jesus was successful because He had the seven success buttons packaged in the Holy Ghost. Everyone who wants to succeed must care to have the Holy Ghost. With Him there is no failure, only success.

When He takes residence in you, He brings along these 7 power-packed spirits that makes destiny fulfilling and successful.

"And the spirit of the Lord shall rest upon him, the spirit of wisdom and understanding, the spirit of counsel and might, the spirit of knowledge and of the fear of the Lord;" (Isaiah 11:2)

- **The Spirit of the Lord.**
He is the power of God- Ye shall receive power (Acts 1:8, 10:38). When He comes He will make you powerful.
"And, behold, I send the promise of my Father upon you: but tarry ye in the city of Jerusalem, until ye be endued with power from on high." (Luke 24:49)

His power helps to silence and dominate the enemy. (Psalm 110:1-3) Power which is the Spirit of the Lord helps you to deal with the enemy so you can have easy access in life. The Holy Spirit brings power to you. The kingdom of God suffers grievous opposition; so you must be empowered! You are a sheep that must be empowered as a lion to deliver destiny. He gives you ability and boldness to silence devils and do great things successfully. *"...Greater is he that is in you than those in the world" (1John 4:4).* So we need Him to overcome all obstacles and clear the road for a smooth ride. In Acts 13:6-12, Elymas the sorcerer wanted to oppose the gospel and Paul filled with the Holy Ghost set his eyes on him and commanded him to be blind. He was blinded instantly. The man believed the gospel. We need power to silence opposition and fulfil destiny.

- **The Spirit of Wisdom.**
Wisdom is God's way of doing things. He brings wisdom into your life. "Wisdom is the principal thing; therefore get wisdom:" (Proverbs 4:7)

Wisdom helps you to choose right and do right. It makes you prosperous as we see in the life of King Solomon (1 Kings 3:3-14). Understand that exploits in life are products of wisdom.

"O Lord, how manifold are thy works! in wisdom hast thou made them all: the earth is full of thy riches." (Psalm 104:24)

HOLY SPIRIT MY PARTNER FOR ALL ROUND SUCCESS

In Ephesians, Paul prayed that God may give to the church the spirit of wisdom (Ephesians 1:17). You can pray for the spirit of wisdom. Wisdom
makes you build things. The scriptures say the end time saints shall build
"And they shall build the old waste..." (Isaiah 61:4). But it takes wisdom to build anything - a church, house, business, etc. *"Through wisdom is*
an house builded; and by understanding it is established:" (Proverbs
24:3)
I see you building churches, houses, businesses and many great things by the spirit of wisdom in Jesus name!

- **The Spirit of understanding.**

He gives you an understanding mind. This helps you to receive the word of God. *"...and with all thy getting get understanding"* (Proverbs 4:7)

We understand from Job 32:8 (AMP) that; *"But there is [a vital force] a spirit [of intelligence] in man, and the breath of the Almighty gives men*
understanding."
Proverbs 2:6 says *"...out of his mouth cometh knowledge and understanding."*
This tells us that Jesus breathing upon the disciples and saying "Receive ye the Holy Ghost...", was to open their understanding: (John 20:22 /
Luke 24:45). This understanding gives you insight into deep things, helping you to grasp concepts, giving you the upper hand. He makes
you outstanding. (Dan 5:11). "Spirit of understanding" is to set you apart for favour.

"Good understanding giveth favour: but the way of transgressors is

hard." *(Proverbs 13:15)*. It makes you stand out of the crowd. It makes you an outstanding personality. No student must fail exams anymore if

they receive the Holy Spirit and engage Him in their studies. He was the spirit behind Daniel's outstanding mental exploit (Dan 5:11).

Paul prayed for us to get it, so you can pray to get it (Eph. 1:16-18). It will help you to know and go for what is yours in redemption.

- **The Spirit of Counsel.**

He provides counsel, advice and directions. He leads us into profitability. If only you listen and follow His lead, you will not go in the wrong direction. He speaks within you.

"And thine ears shall hear a word behind thee, saying, This is the way, walk ye in it, when ye turn to the right hand, and when ye turn to the left." (Isaiah 30:21)

"Thus saith the Lord, thy Redeemer, the Holy One of Israel; I am the Lord thy God which teacheth thee to profit, which leadeth thee by the

way that thou shouldest go." (Isaiah 48:17)

In Acts 13:2-4, the Holy Spirit directed the apostles to choose and send Paul and Barnabas to Antioch. We see the Spirit of counsel leading the

early church and advising them into God's perfect purpose to ensure their victory.

- **The Spirit of Might.**

Inner strength, energy and stamina to keep going without fainting. Strong body, devoid of sickness and weakness.

"For this cause I bow my knees unto the Father of our Lord Jesus Christ, Of whom the whole family in heaven and earth is named,

that he would grant you, according to the riches of his glory, to be strengthened with might by his Spirit in the inner man;" (Ephesians 3:14-16)

HOLY SPIRIT MY PARTNER FOR ALL ROUND SUCCESS

You need to "run" with vision (Hab 2:2). So you need strength to run the race of life successfully. (Isaiah 40:29-31).

The Holy Spirit invigorates our mortal bodies thereby destroying weakness and sickness.

"But if the Spirit of him that raised up Jesus from the dead dwell in you, he that raised up Christ from the dead shall also quicken your mortal bodies by his Spirit that dwelleth in you." (Romans 8:11)

May you receive healing and strength right now as you are reading this

book in the name of Jesus.

- **The Spirit of Knowledge.**

Light is vital and supreme in the conflict of life. You need knowledge to triumph in life. (Hosea 4:6). You need to know how to prosper, marry, raise Godly children, have a successful business and live long etc. And all these happen by knowledge (revelation). *"You shall 'know' the truth..." (John 8:32)*

Every man's freedom is determined by his level of knowledge. The Holy Spirit teaches us all things.

"But the Comforter, which is the Holy Ghost, whom the Father will send in my name, he shall teach you all things, and bring all things to your remembrance, whatsoever I have said unto you." (John 14:26)

This spirit will let you know deep things that ordinary people do not know (1 Cor. :10-11). Through the Holy Spirit, we are able to know the word of God. God is no more a mystery to us, as some other religions see Him. the Holy Spirit reveals things to us.

"Now we have received, not the spirit of the world, but the spirit which is of God; that we might know the things that are freely given to us of God. Which things also we speak, not in the words which man's wisdom teacheth, but which the Holy Ghost teacheth; comparing spiritual things with spiritual." (1 Corinthians 2:12-13).

- **Spirit of the fear of God.**

The fear of God will bring you into unprecedented and unexplainable exploits and record-breaking achievements.

- That was the secret of Joseph's greatness. *"For I fear God."* (Gen 42:18)

- It was the secret of Job's greatness. (Job 1:8) *"Then Satan answered the Lord, and said, Doth Job fear God for nought?" (Job 1:9)*

The devil will not fear you until you fear God. Men will fear you when you fear God. It makes you untouchable because the fear of God makes you a carrier of the presence of God all the time.

"And who is he that will harm you, if ye be followers of that which is good?" (1 Peter 3:13)

It is the spirit of holiness that causes God to have an unbroken partnership with you.

"And if God be for you ...who can be against you." (Rom 8:31).

We must pray for the manifestation of the seven spirits in our lives so we can win like Jesus. The fear of God is your guaranteed access to heaven. Your gifts are good but they do not guarantee you access to heaven. The fear of God that makes you live without sin, is the access key.

These are the ingredients of success and they come by the Holy Ghost. It is dangerous to live without the Holy Ghost. Every believer must have the baptism of the Holy Ghost with evidence of speaking in tongues (Acts 2:4).

HOW TO ENCOUNTER THE SEVEN (7) SPIRITS OF GOD

You need to fellowship with Him so that His anointing in these seven ways will rub on you continuously in increasing measure.

Chapter 6
Manifestations Of The Spirit

When the Holy Spirit is in a man's life, He manifests Himself in so many ways and brings so many blessings in that man's life. These are some of

His blessings:
- **He brings power into your life.**

When you receive the Holy Spirit you simply receive the power of God for conquest (Acts 1:8, Acts 10:38, Luke 24:49). Put simply, to walk in

dominion over all powers of darkness. This power helps us to fulfil the most important mission of the Holy Spirit, which is soul winning. He

empowers us to win souls into the kingdom. Soul winning is the principal ministry of the Holy Ghost and therefore when you are filled with His power, you will be an addicted soul winner.

"But ye shall receive power, after that the Holy Ghost is come upon you: and ye shall be witnesses unto me both in Jerusalem, and in all Judaea, and in Samaria, and unto the uttermost part of the earth." (Acts 1:8)

If you are not a soul winner, the power of God in your life will soon run out because of lack of use. To enjoy His power continuously, be a soul winner.

- He brings God's presence.

The Holy Spirit brings God's presence in your life. He is called "The Angel of God's presence." He is the conveyor or messenger of God's presence.

"In all their affliction he was afflicted, and the angel of his presence saved

them: in his love and in his pity he redeemed them; and he bare them, and carried them all the days of old. But they rebelled, and vexed his Holy Spirit: therefore he was turned to be their enemy, and he fought against them." (Isaiah 63:9-10)

The Holy Spirit manifests God's presence and brings to us the awareness of the power of God. He makes God's presence real to us and that reality stirs up faith in us, which is necessary to provoke the miraculous. Wherever 'the Angel of His presence' visits, there are miracles, healings, signs and wonders. Understand that God is omnipresent but His manifest presence is not everywhere. David knowing the importance of God's presence cried out *"Do not cast me away from your presence, and do not take your Holy Spirit from me" (Psalm 51:11 NKJV).*

This same presence brings joy to the heart of the believer (Psalm 16:11). It is my prayer that you enjoy the presence of God all the days of your life by the ministry of the Holy Ghost.

- **He gives you rest.**

The Holy Ghost will give you rest from troubles. There could be trouble and confusion all around your environment. When the Holy Spirit is in you in His fullness, He will give you peace and rest. Jesus came to give you rest. *"Come unto me, all ye that labour and are heavy laden, and I will give you rest." (Matthew 11:28)*

This was Jesus speaking, and the Holy Spirit has come to continue the ministry from where He (Jesus) left off. The Holy Ghost is doing in us, the same thing Jesus did while on earth.

"But the Comforter, which is the Holy Ghost, whom the Father will send

HOLY SPIRIT MY PARTNER FOR ALL ROUND SUCCESS

in my name, he shall teach you all things, and bring all things to your remembrance, whatsoever I have said unto you. "Peace I leave with you, my peace I give unto you: not as the world giveth, give I unto you. Let

not your heart be troubled, neither let it be afraid." (John 14:26-27)

When you are filled with the Holy Spirit, anxiety has no power over you.

You are always restful no matter the bad news. You sleep soundly in the midst of trouble. *"When men are cast down, then thou shalt say, there*

is lifting up..."(Job 22:29).

When you are full of the Holy Ghost, fear loses its power over you. He calms your spirit and brings rest to your soul. You enjoy heavenly peace on earth.

- **He makes you beautiful.**

The Holy Spirit is the beauty of Christianity. He comes into our lives and brings the beauty of heaven.

"By his spirit has he garnished the heavens..." (Job 26:13 KJV) *"The heavens are made beautiful by his Spirit;..."* (Job 26:13 TLB)

Anyone filled with the Holy Spirit always looks glorious. Glory means beauty. The Holy Ghost is referred to as, 'the glory of the Father' (Romans 6:4, 8:11). He gives colour to destiny. His anointing makes us beautiful and attractive. The prophet Isaiah speaking about the Holy Ghost said' *"...to give unto them beauty for Ashes."* (Isaiah 61:3)

I therefore decree by the Holy Ghost that every shame in your life is terminated in Jesus name!

- **He teaches you.**

One of the profound things the Holy Ghost does for the church is to teach us. He is your teacher. Anytime you find any subject difficult to understand, just call on Him saying, "Holy Spirit open my mind and teach me now in Jesus' name!" He teaches the word of God so we will not walk in darkness (John 8:12).

He reveals the mysteries behind the word of God to us.

"But the Comforter, which is the Holy Ghost, whom the Father will send in my name, he shall teach you all things, and bring all things to your remembrance, whatsoever I have said unto you." (John 14:26)

The Holy Spirit, is called 'the spirit of truth', which means reality. This means He is the only one that can really open your eyes to the truth concerning any subject in life.

"Howbeit when he, the Spirit of truth, is come, he will guide you into all truth: for he shall not speak of himself; but whatsoever he shall hear, that shall he speak: and he will shew you things to come. He shall glorify me: for he shall receive of mine, and shall shew it unto you." (John 16:13- 14)

The Holy Spirit is also the custodian of divine secrets, He receives from Jesus and makes it plain to us. In other words, He is the master teacher.

He wrote the Bible and so He is the best interpreter of the book.

"For the prophecy came not in old time by the will of man: but holy men of God spake as they were moved by the Holy Ghost." (2 Peter 1:21)

Until you engage His services during your studies, you may read but you will not understand for your profiting. Always call on Him when you are studying and He will teach you all things.

- **He refreshes, renews and restores you.**

When The Holy Spirit takes residence in you, He will make sure your power and abilities do not run out.

"The Lord is my shepherd; I shall not want. He maketh me to lie down in green pastures: he leadeth me beside the still waters. He restoreth my soul: he leadeth me in the paths of righteousness for his name's sake." (Psalms 23:1-3)

HOLY SPIRIT MY PARTNER FOR ALL ROUND SUCCESS

David by saying the lord is my shepherd is sharing with us his revelation
about the Holy Spirit. *"...The Lord is that Spirit..." (2 Cor. 3:17).* We are told again that the Holy Spirit is the Shepherd of our souls (1 Peter 2:25).

He reveals to us that when the Spirit comes to dwell in us, nothing will grow old because the Holy Spirit renews our strength: *"who satisfieth*
thy mouth with good things so that thy youth is renewed like the eagle's."
(Ps. 103:5) "And he shall be like a tree planted by rivers of water, that bringeth forth
his fruit in his season; his leaf shall not wither(not run dry)..." (Ps 1:3)

The men who knew the Holy Ghost never grew weak or old:
- Moses was climbing mountains at 120 years with no dimness of eyes nor weakness of body (Deut. 34:1&7)
- Caleb at 85 years said he was as strong as he was at 40. At 85 he was still fighting to possess lands to start new projects. (Joshua 14:6-13).
- Papa Hagin at 86 was still preaching, dancing and shouting.
- Dr. Kenneth Copeland is still preaching and running on the pulpit at 80. *"For which cause we faint not; but though our outward man perish,*
yet the inward man is renewed day by day." (2 Corinthians 4:16)

Refuse to grow old or retire! Refuse to die by accident, sickness or gunshot! You must 'go home' full of age, strength and vitality at God's
time, when you have fully finished God's will for you on earth. Declare
"I am getting stronger by the day, I have renewed strength in the Holy Ghost!" Nothing runs dry because the Holy Spirit refreshes us.

"Repent ye therefore, and be converted, that your sins may be blotted

out, *when the times of refreshing shall come from the presence of the Lord;" (Acts 3:19)*

The Apostle Peter was preaching on the day of Pentecost and said, after one has repented and become a child of God, refreshing will come from

God's presence. He was referring to the refreshing that comes with the Holy Spirit. The pleasure and joy that comes with His presence. (Ps 16:11). This means when the Holy Ghost takes His abode in you, He refreshes you all the time. You can't burn out with stress! Praise God! Halleluyah!

If you don't have the Holy Spirit, you need Him now! Because without Him you will lose steam and energy. I decree right now be filled and be

refilled with the Holy Spirit in the name of Jesus! When you are full of the Holy Spirit, you enjoy 'season-free' strength and vitality to keep you

going all the days of your life. His presence refreshes us. No room for dryness, stress and heaviness. We cannot be drained physically,

spiritually, mentally or financially. He will always supply us with something fresh. Glory to God!

Nothing is lost because the Holy Spirit restores you. We are told in Joel about the Holy Ghost; *"And I will restore to you the years that the locust*

hath eaten, the cankerworm, and the caterpiller, and the palmerworm, my great army which I sent among you." (Joel 2:25)

When He takes His place in you, He becomes your standby to restore power when the natural power runs out of supply. (Comforter- 'Allos

parakletos', just like Jesus. He restores anything lost or dead. He is our standby -John 16:7)

HOLY SPIRIT MY PARTNER FOR ALL ROUND SUCCESS

We see the Holy Ghost bringing God's presence for miracles, renewal, refreshment and restoration. This is why Paul says be, "filled with the
Holy Ghost", so you can enjoy miracles, renewal, refreshing and restoration.

- **He empowers you for righteousness.**

The Holy Spirit helps you to live right. We call him the Holy Spirit, so when he comes to dwell in you, he produces His fruits of Holiness in
you. As unclean spirits make people unclean so does the Holy Spirit make people holy. Many Christians struggle with many evil habits. They want to stop drinking alcohol, stealing, telling lies, fighting, cheating and even fornicating. Some have problems with laziness and even eating too much. The Holy Spirit is there to help you drop those destructive habits. All you need is to be full of His presence. When you are full of the Holy
Ghost through prayer and speaking in tongues, His ability will be stirred in you to break the power of those evil habits. He will help you to do the
things that please God.

"For it is God which worketh in you both to will and to do of his good pleasure." (Philippians 2:13)

This means the Holy Spirit will make you willing and can make you do
what is right. Therefore the struggle to do right comes to an end when you recognize that the Holy Spirit is there to empower you to do right.

Scripture says, *"And ye shall receive power..."(Acts 1:8)*. The word power
here is translated from the Greek word 'Dunamis'. It is also translated as 'the dynamic ability to cause changes'. So when the Holy Ghost comes
into you, He gives you power (the dynamic ability to cause changes).
This means you can cause changes in your behaviour and character as

well as other areas of your life. Anything you do not want, you have the ability to change it. You are not helpless and powerless in any situation.

You can always make desired changes because the ability to do what is right has been imparted into your spirit. Holiness is the nature of God, so when you receive His Spirit, you can now produce the fruit of His nature. You can now stand before God without any sense of guilt, inferiority or condemnation. The presence of the Holy Spirit in you, is your ability to produce righteousness. As you are reading this book, every bad habit or addiction is losing its power over you in the name of Jesus! Anytime you feel a strong urge to do something wrong, just speak

in tongues till you are overpowered by God's presence. When your spirit is charged up, it will suppress all evil desires of your flesh.

- **He makes you very fruitful.**

The Holy Spirit is a life giving spirit; so His presence gives life to everything around. Barrenness, dryness and unfruitfulness cannot survive around the Holy Spirit.

"And the Lord God formed man of the dust of the ground, and breathed into his nostrils the breath of life; and man became a living soul." (Genesis 2:7)

We see that life began with the breath of God from the very beginning. His breath is His Spirit. So fruitfulness is tied to the Holy Spirit. Some

churches, business and individuals are experiencing dryness. The solution to their dryness is the Holy Spirit. When you allow Him to come

and fill you up, your season of dryness expires.

"Until the spirit be poured upon us from on high, and the wilderness

be a fruitful field, and the fruitful field be counted for a forest. Then *judgment shall dwell in the wilderness, and righteousness remain in the fruitful field" (Isaiah 32:15-16)*

This scripture opens us up to another ministry of the Holy Spirit. His presence and influence makes everything productive. He will make your mind productive as a student to scale academic heights. He will make a barren woman productive to have children. He will make a ministry productive to have church growth. Wherever things are going bad and dry, His presence will make all the difference. The Bible says *"...until the spirit be poured from on high..."* His spirit turns the wilderness into a fruitful field and the fruitful field into a forest. Remember fruitfulness is in degrees. Some have churches of less than fifty, some have hundreds, others thousands, some tens of thousands and some above a million.

Who is responsible for that? The Holy Spirit. He is the Lord of the harvest.

"Pray ye therefore the Lord of the harvest that he will send forth labourers into his harvest." (Matthew 9:38)

We are told to pray so that he can give us increase. It is impossible to overcome dryness and see increase without the involvement of the Holy Spirit. This suggests that we need Him more than ever before. When He comes to dwell in us, our season of fruitfulness begins.

Let us be continuously filled with the Holy Spirit through speaking in tongues so we can enjoy fruitfulness every day. Fruitfulness is also prosperity: You must take note that fruitfulness also has to do with prosperity. The anointing of the Holy Spirit makes us financially productive.

"And I will put my spirit within you, and cause you to walk in my statutes, and ye shall keep my judgments, and do them. And ye shall dwell in the land that I gave to your fathers; and ye shall be my

people, and I will be your God. I will also save you from all your uncleannesses: and I will call for the corn, and will increase it, and lay no famine upon you. And I will multiply the fruit of the tree, and the increase of the field, that ye shall receive no more reproach of famine among the heathen." (Ezekiel 36:27-30)

God is telling us that He will put His Spirit within us and as a result, every curse and mess will be taken away. He will give us corn (prosperity) and take famine (poverty) away. Many Christians are broke

and empty, but the Holy Spirit is the answer. Prosperity comes by the Holy Ghost. He is the one that waters our 'seeds' and brings in the

'harvest'. After 'sowing your seed', spend time to pray and speak in tongues. Prayer makes the rain to fall on your seed. Here the rain is the

Holy Spirit and He responds to prayer. Everything done by the Holy Ghost can be

demanded on the altar of prayer. In Zechariah 10:1, we are told to ask of the Lord for the latter rain. He is the one who comes to water our

seeds for harvest. We have already received the baptism of the Holy Ghost; so let us engage Him in prayer to prove His fruitfulness and

prosperity.

- **He makes you excellent.**

The Holy Spirit is the spirit of excellence. He influences you to do excellent things. He causes you to excel and to go beyond human

limitations. We are told in scriptures that Daniel excelled above his companions because he had an excellent spirit.

"Then this Daniel was preferred above the presidents and princes, be- cause an excellent spirit was in him; and the king thought to set him over the whole realm." (Daniel 6:3)

This means there is a spirit of excellence that causes men to excel. Everyone that received the Holy Spirit received excellence in His Spirit.

All you need is to allow the Holy Ghost to express himself through you. You become an excellent student, businessman, pastor, wife, husband,

HOLY SPIRIT MY PARTNER FOR ALL ROUND SUCCESS

singer etc. You do well in all things (Ps 1:3). You begin to do things to perfection through the Holy Spirit dwelling in you (Ps 138:8).

With the spirit of excellence, your mistakes and errors are minimized. You do things with the touch of class. When you pray in the Holy Ghost,

the spirit of excellence comes out to affect you physically, mentality, financially, spiritually and in all other areas. Your life becomes attractive and prosperous. You begin to influence people and things because excellence is attractive and charming. That will be your story from this day forward by the help of the Holy Spirit within you!

- **He makes you anointed.**

If you see anointing anywhere, it is the work of the Holy Ghost. He is the only one that anoints. Even Jesus was anointed by the Holy Ghost (Acts 10:38). For any other person to be anointed he needs to walk in close fellowship with the Holy Spirit.

- **He guides you into success.**

The Holy Spirit is a guide, He leads and He guides into all truth. He makes all things real to you. *"Howbeit when he, the Spirit of truth, is come, he will guide you into all truth: for he shall not speak of himself; but whatsoever he shall hear, that shall he speak: and he will shew you*

things to come." (John 16:13)

With Him as your companion, the road always looks good. He will guide

you into the right ministry, the right marriage partner, the right and profitable business and the right places. You will not regret the decisions taken. The man without the Holy Spirit is like an aircraft without a pilot and a sheep without a shepherd. The Holy Spirit gives us a sense of direction. Without Him, life is a struggle in darkness. Every child of God is entitled to His guidance that guarantees a struggle-free and stress-free life.

"For as many as are led by the spirit of God, they are the sons of God.
(Romans 8:14)
Children of God are not led by their physical senses but by the Spirit. Since the Spirit searches all things (I Cor. 2:10), those who are guided by the Spirit do not struggle in life because He shows them the right way to make it easily in life. By the Holy Spirit that dwells in you, may you enjoy His guidance in all areas of your life!

- **He brings healing to you.**

Every child of God is entitled to the healing ministry of the Holy Spirit. When the Spirit comes to dwell in you, His power travels through your veins, blood and all parts of your body. His indwelling presence gives you power to overcome devils of sicknesses, diseases and infirmities. He is in you to give life to your mortal body.

"But if the Spirit of him that raised up Jesus from the dead dwell in you, he that raised up Christ from the dead shall also quicken your mortal bodies by his Spirit that dwelleth in you." (Romans 8:11)

When did He give life to your mortal body?

The very day He took residence in you, He vitalized your mortal body. In case you are attacked by any sickness or disease just remember you have 'the healer' in you. Turn to Him to do the job. Refuse to die by sickness or disease. The Holy Spirit is in you to vitalize, energize and invigorate your weak or dead body. We are told in that same scripture that it was the Holy Ghost who raised up Jesus from the dead. This means resurrection power resides in all believers who have the Holy Ghost. Therefore in case you are sick whiles reading this book, I command you to be healed instantly in the name of Jesus! I demand and command

your healing now. Get up and speak in tongues till your whole being is inundated, saturated and overflowing with the Holy Spirit. Activate the
healing power by praying in tongues. Refuse to be sick or weak. We are told by scripture that when Moses was 120 years of age, he had
no sight problems or physical weakness. (Deut 34:7). Moses did not have the Holy Ghost dwelling in him like those of us in the New Testament,
but upon him. If he was climbing mountains at 120 years without pains, aches and weaknesses, then we have better opportunities in the New Testament.

Because His Spirit lives in us, anything that destroys will be destroyed by the Holy Spirit. (1 Cor 3:16 -17)

If you are filled with the Holy Spirit, then the He lives and walks in you (2 Cor. 6:16). He guards your body against encroachment of terminal diseases, HIV, tuberculosis and all forms of deadly sicknesses and diseases.

Chapter 7

SPEAKING IN TONGUES
(As evidence of the baptism of the Holy Spirit)

The Holy Spirit is the exclusive preserve of children of God. It is a kingdom virtue for kingdom people. To receive the Holy Spirit, you must first be born again! (John 3:3). If you are not sure you are saved, pray this prayer right now and receive Jesus into your life based on Romans 10:9&10.

Prayer of Salvation

"Father, I believe with my heart that Jesus died for me. I confess with my mouth that Jesus is Lord. My sins are forgiven. You are my Lord and personal saviour. I am born again in the name of Jesus!"

If you have prayed this prayer, then you are a child of God! Every born again child of God is entitled to receive the Holy Spirit with the evidence of speaking in tongues. Peter, when preaching on the day of Pentecost said; *"But this is that which was spoken by the prophet Joel; And it shall come to pass in the last days, saith God, I will pour out of my Spirit upon all flesh: and your sons and your daughters shall prophesy, and your young men shall see visions, and your old men shall dream dreams:"(Acts 2:16-17)*

No matter which denomination you belong to, the Bible is our standard. However, the Holy Spirit does not force Himself on anyone except the person believes the word and acts on it by expressing his or her desire to receive the Holy Spirit baptism with the evidence of speaking in tongues.

HOLY SPIRIT MY PARTNER FOR ALL ROUND SUCCESS

"And they were all filled with the Holy Ghost, and began to speak with other tongues, as the Spirit gave them utterance." (Acts 2:4)

Many are teaching that it is enough to have the Holy Spirit without speaking in tongues. The truth is in Acts 2:4. The Bible says they that received the Holy Spirit 'began to speak in tongues'. That is the Biblical truth. It cancels any church doctrine that goes contrary to the scripture! You receive power when the Holy Spirit comes into you life (Acts 1:8).

This means you are powerless if He is not in your life. It is to your own advantage as a child of God to desire the infilling of the Holy Spirit.

Without Him, you lose all the amazing blessings I have shared in this book.

In case you are born again and you still have not received the Holy Spirit, just pray and say; "Father, you love me and sent Jesus to die for me. Now

that I believe in Jesus, I have the right to receive the Holy Spirit with the evidence of speaking in tongues. I receive the Holy Spirit now into my

spirit in the name of Jesus."

The Blessings of Speaking in Tongues

- **When you pray in tongues you are edified.** It builds up the believer

spiritually.

"He that speaketh in an unknown tongue edifieth himself; but he that prophesieth edifieth the church." (1 Corinthians 14:4)

- **When tongues are spoken with interpretation, the church is also edified.**

"I would that ye all spake with tongues, but rather that ye prophesied: for greater is he that prophesieth than he that speaketh with tongues, except he interpret, that the church may receive edifying." (1 Corinthians 14:5)

- **Speaking in tongues is a sign that God's Spirit is dwelling in you.**

"And they were all filled with the Holy Ghost, and began to speak with other tongues, as the Spirit gave them utterance."

- **Speaking in tongues is speaking spiritual mysteries (divine secrets).**

It means you communicate with the supernatural God in a supernatural language!

"For he that speaketh in an unknown tongue speaketh not unto men, but unto God: for no man understandeth him; howbeit in the spirit he speaketh mysteries." (1 Corinthians 14:2)

- **Praying in tongues helps you to pray in line with Gods perfect will.** *"Likewise the Spirit also helpeth our infirmities: for we know not what we should pray for as we ought: but the Spirit itself maketh intercession for us with groanings which cannot be uttered."* **(Romans 8:26)**

That agrees with what Paul said in 1 Corinthians 14:14, *"For if I pray in an unknown tongue, my spirit prayeth, but my understanding is unfruitful."* **Warning:** People should be careful about making fun of speaking in tongues, because when a person prays in tongues, it is his spirit praying by the Holy Spirit who is within him. Thus, mockers actually are making fun of the Holy Spirit! The Holy Spirit within you gives you the utterance; you speak it out of your spirit. Therefore the Holy Spirit helps you pray according to the will of God for things that should be prayed for.

- **Praying in tongues stirs up faith in you.**

Speaking in tongues helps me to learn to trust God more fully. It helps my faith to speak in tongues. It will not give me faith; but rather helps my faith!

"But ye, beloved, building up yourselves on your most holy faith, praying in the Holy Ghost..." (Jude 20)

HOLY SPIRIT MY PARTNER FOR ALL ROUND SUCCESS

Here is conclusive proof. Praying in tongues helps and stimulates my faith. You receive Holy Ghost boldness and faith to do exploits and face any challenge.

- **Praying in tongues keeps your mind on God and keeps you away from secular contamination.** When you find yourself in a public place where dirty and profane words are spoken or music is playing, you can speak in tongues undertone (under your voice). That will keep your mind from wandering and being contaminated. Regardless of where you may be, you can do as 1 Corinthians 14:28 says, *"...and let him speak to himself, and to God."* You can do this to keep your mind on God in public without disturbing anyone.

- **Praying in tongues helps you to pray for the unknown.**

It enables you to take care of the unforeseen future. It covers the blind spots of your life. Speaking in tongues provides a way for situations to be prayed for that no one knows or thinks about. The Holy Spirit, on the other hand, knows everything. The Word of God says, *"...But the Spirit itself maketh intercession for us with groanings which cannot be uttered"*
(Romans 8:26)

- **Praying in tongues refreshes you.**

We are living in a world full of challenges and troubles that bring stress, frustration and insecurity to the masses. Speaking in tongues is the best way to rest your soul. It refreshes your entire system body, soul and spirit.

"For with stammering lips and another tongue will he speak to this people. To whom he said, This is the rest wherewith ye may cause the weary to rest; and this is the refreshing: yet they would not hear."
(Isaiah 28:11-12)

- **Praying in the spirit is the best and perfect way of thanking God.**

The more you thank God, the more He increases you in everything. It is vital to thank him perfectly, and speaking in tongues gets it done!

"What is it then? I will pray with the spirit, and also...I will sing with the spirit...For thou verily givest thanks well..." (1 Corinthians 14:15- 17)

Keep being filled with the Spirit

After receiving the baptism of the Holy Ghost with the evidence of speaking in tongues, you can grow in the spirit by daily praying and

singing in the Holy Spirit. It will help you to be full of the Holy Spirit always to meet the challenges of everyday life - fully prepared to win.

Paul said in 1Corinthians 14:15, *"I will pray with the spirit... I will sing with the spirit..."*

Every Spirit-filled believer should be doing that every day in his private

prayer life. Unless we are doing it, we are not keeping ourselves filled with the Spirit.

Chapter 8

The Gifts Of The Holy Spirit

The nine gifts of the Holy Spirit are a result of the Holy Spirit's infilling power. The nine fruits of the Holy Spirit are a result of the Holy Spirit's
indwelling presence.

THE GIFTS OF THE SPIRIT

The Holy Spirit has gifts for the whole body of Christ. These are supernatural gifts that enhance the effectiveness of the body of Christ.

They are nine in all. We will discuss them briefly.

"Now there are diversities of gifts, but the same Spirit. And there are differences of administrations, but the same Lord. And there are diversities of operations, but it is the same God which worketh all in all. But the manifestation of the Spirit is given to every man to profit withal. For to one is given by the Spirit the word of wisdom; to another the word of knowledge by the same Spirit; To another faith by the same Spirit; to another the gifts of healing by the same Spirit;

To another the working of miracles; to another prophecy; to another discerning of spirits; to another divers kinds of tongues; to another

the interpretation of tongues: But all these worketh that one and the selfsame Spirit, dividing to every man severally as he will." (1 Corinthians 12:4-11)

From the scriptures we see that the gifts may differ in function and operation but they come from the same Holy Spirit. These nine gifts are broken into three different categories for effective working:

Three revelation gifts: These are spiritual gifts that reveal something: the word of wisdom, the word of knowledge and the discerning of spirits.

Three power gifts: These are spiritual gifts that do something: gift of faith, the working of miracles and the gifts of healing. **Three utterance or inspirational gifts;** These are spiritual gifts that say something: the gift of prophecy, divers kinds of tongues and interpretation of tongues.

REVELATION GIFTS

- **The Word of Kisdom.**

The word of wisdom is a supernatural revelation by the Spirit of God concerning the divine purposes and plans in the mind and will of God and it is the best gift. It is different from the word of knowledge. While
the word of knowledge also brings revelation, this revelation is always about the present or concerns things that have happened in the past. On
the other hand, the word of wisdom always speaks of the future.

- **The Word of Knowledge.**

The word of knowledge is the supernatural revelation by the Holy Ghost of certain facts in the mind of God. Facts about people, places or things
in the past or present. God is all-knowing. He knows everything. But He does not reveal everything He knows to man. He just gives him a
word or a part of what He knows. A word is a fragmentary part of a sentence, so a word of knowledge would simply be a fragmentary part
of the entire knowledge or counsel of God. God has all knowledge. But He does not impart all of His knowledge to us; He imparts a word of
knowledge to us — just what He wants us to know at a given time. Most often, the gift of the word of wisdom and the gift of the word of
knowledge work together (Acts 21:10-13).

- **Discerning of spirits.**

The discerning of spirits gives supernatural insight into the spirit world. "To discern" means to perceive by seeing or hearing. Therefore, discerning of spirits is the same as seeing or hearing in the realms of the spirit. This gift actually has a more limited range of operation than the other two revelation gifts. It gives us supernatural insight only into the

realms of the spirit. It also reveals the kind of spirit that is in operation behind a supernatural manifestation. The discerning of spirits is not the

discerning of character or faults; it is not even the discerning of people. It is called the discerning of spirits, and it deals with spirits that exist in

the spirit realm, whether they are divine, satanic, or human (Acts 16:16-18).

POWER GIFTS
- **The Gift of Faith**

It is a supernatural manifestation of the Holy Spirit whereby a believer is empowered with special faith or wonder-working faith. It is beyond

simple saving faith which brings one to salvation. The gift of faith is the greatest of the three power gifts! This gift is miraculous just as the rest

of the gifts of the Spirit are miraculous.

The gift of faith is a gift of the Holy Spirit to the believer in order that he might receive miracles. It is a special gift which is given supernaturally

by the Spirit of God, as He wills. Those who operate in this special faith can believe God in such a way that God honors their words as His own,

and miraculously brings to pass their desired results. The gift of faith can operate to cast out demons, to receive the dead raised back to life, and to supernaturally sustain a person beyond the ability of ordinary faith. Remember, ordinary faith comes by hearing the Word of God

(Rom. 10:17). But the gift of faith is manifested by the Holy Spirit to enable a person to receive a miracle beyond the capacity that ordinary faith can receive. Throughout the Bible we see how the gift of faith worked primarily for people who were in danger. And through this gift of the Spirit, they possessed a calmness and quiet assurance that was supernatural. Daniel received deliverance from lions by the gift of faith.(Daniel 6:23). Papa Hagin and Benson Idahosa (all of blessed memory) operated the gift of faith. In our days, my father Bishop David Oyedepo is known around the world as a man of this awesome gift of faith (receiving the baton-transfer of the gift from Papa Hagin) and the proofs are evident. We need this gift in increasing dimension to succeed in life and ministry.

All these come from the Holy Spirit. Receive your portion of the gift of faith in Jesus name!

- **The Working of Miracles**

A miracle can be defined as a supernatural intervention by God in the ordinary course of nature. When this gift is in manifestation, there is a divine intervention in the ordinary course of nature. For example, the dividing of a stream by the sweep of a mantle is an example of the gift of working of miracles in operation (2 Kings 2:14). After Elijah ascended to heaven in a chariot in the whirlwind, Elisha received his mantle and smote the Jordan River with it, dividing the waters. This brought an interruption in the natural flow of the river, thus a miracle occurred! Jesus also operated in this gift when He turned water into wine in John 2:1-11.

A miracle therefore, is a temporary suspension of the accustomed order, or an interruption in the system of nature operated by the power of the

Holy Spirit. Reading from the writings of Rev Kenneth Hagin Sr, I discovered that the difference between the gift of faith and the working of miracles is that the gift of faith receives a miracle and the working of miracles works a miracle. The working of miracles is used to display God's power and magnificence. In Young's Analytical Concordance to the Bible, the Greek word for "miracles" in 1 Corinthians 12:10 is *"dunamis,"* and can also be translated as the acts of powers. In other words, the working of miracles could also be called the working of acts of powers. According to the Greek concordance, the Greek word also means explosions of almightiness or impelling, staggering wonders or astonishments. It is simply a display of God's almighty power. Paul was said to have worked miracles (Acts 19:7). Stephen also did great wonders and miracles. All these are manifestations of the gift of working of miracles in the New Testament. We need gifts in our days to change our world. Through the working of miracles, loaves were multiplied (Matt 14:17-21; Mark 6:38-44; Luke 9:13-17; John 6:9-14), a solid iron axe head was made to float in water as if it were a piece of wood (2 Kings 6:5-7), the raging force of a storm was quieted (Mark 4:37-41; Luke 8:23-25), a multitude of fishes filled the disciples' net when they let it down at Jesus' instruction (John 21:6-8,11), the widow's small pot of oil became a fountain of oil and provided sustenance for her and her son (2 Kings 4:1-7). The gift of working of miracles is for us today. Receive in it in Jesus name. It is my prayer that the church will flow in such gifts in these last days.

- **The Gifts of Healing**

The gifts of healing are manifested for the supernatural healing of sicknesses and diseases without any natural source or means. It must be noted that every one of these nine gifts of the Spirit are supernatural. I want to emphasize the supernatural character of the gifts of healing. The gifts of healing have nothing to do with medical science or human learning. Doctors and medical science are natural means of healing. We thank God for medical science and its role in curative medicine. However, this gift of healing is supernatural and doesn't come by diagnosis or by prescribing treatment. Divine healing comes by laying on of hands, anointing with oil, or sometimes just by speaking the Word.

Jesus ministered healing by the Holy Ghost all the time in His ministry. Peter tells us in Acts 10:38..." **How God anointed Jesus with the Holy**

Ghost and power who went about doing good and healing..."

We know, first of all, that the purpose of this gift is to deliver the sick and to destroy the works of the devil in the human body. In our days many were specially anointed with the gift of healing to help the body of Christ; John Alexander Darwin, Kathryn Kuhlman, Kenneth T. Hagin, TL Osborn, Oral Robert all of blessed memory. We also have Kenneth Copeland, Benny Hinn, Pastor Chris Oyakhilome, Bishop Agyin Asare and many others who are alive today ministering healing with the gift of healing to their generation. I have personally recognized this gift operating in my ministry by the kinds of healings taking place in our services.

However, that still does not eliminate receiving healing on your own by simple faith in God's word because the Bible says, *". . . by whose [Jesus']*

stripes ye were healed" (1 Peter 2:24). Thank God for His word and for the privilege of believing and acting upon His word. Apart from healing by faith (receiving healing by standing on the promises of God's word) which is general in the body of Christ, we need the supernatural gift of

healing given by the Holy Ghost to heal the sick because our society today is plagued with so many sickness and diseases that defy medical science. May God grant the church the gifts of healing in the mighty name of

Jesus! If you are reading this book and you are sick, I decree right now, be healed by the power of the Holy Ghost in Jesus name! Receive by

saying Amen!

THE GIFTS OF UTTERANCE

• **The Gift of Prophecy.**

Prophecy is supernatural utterance in a known tongue. The Bible says,

"...greater is he that prophesieth than he that speaketh with tongues,

except he interpret ..." (1 Cor. 14:5).

We infer from this, that to speak with tongues and to interpret the tongues is equivalent to prophecy. Therefore, prophecy is really the most important of these three gifts of inspiration or utterance in that it does not require another gift to complete it. The simple gift of prophecy should not be confused with the prophetic office or with prophetic utterance that may come forth in the prophet's ministry. Paul said, "But he that prophesieth speaketh unto men to edification and exhortation and comfort" (1 Cor. 14:3).

• **Diverse Kinds of Tongues**

This is supernatural utterance in an unknown tongue. It is supernatural utterance by the Holy Spirit in languages never learned by the speaker, understood by the speaker, nor necessarily always understood by the hearer. Speaking with tongues has nothing whatsoever to do with linguistic ability; it has nothing to do with the mind or the intellect of man. It is a vocal miracle of the Holy Spirit.

• **Interpretation of Tongues**

The interpretation of tongues is the supernatural showing forth of the meaning of an utterance in other tongues by the Holy Spirit. It is not the translation of tongues but the interpretation of tongues. It is the least gift of all the gifts of the Holy Spirit because it depends on another gift (diverse kinds of tongues), in order to operate. It does not operate unless tongues have been in operation. The purpose of the gift of interpretation of tongues is to render the gift of tongues understandable to the hearers so that the whole church congregation, as well as the one who gave the utterance in an unknown tongue, may know what has been said and may be edified thereby.

After Paul listed the nine gifts of the Spirit as shown in the text above, he went on to say; *"But covet earnestly the best gifts . . ."*(1Cor. 12:31).

The 'best' gift is the gift needed at the time. According to Papa Hagin in his teachings, people sometimes become confused about what the best spiritual gift is. They miss the fact that under some circumstances, even the very best gift of all the spiritual gifts, may not be the best gift in a given circumstance or the gift needed at that particular time. For instance, the word of wisdom is the greatest of all the gifts of the Spirit. However, if you are sick, you don't need that manifestation; you need a manifestation of the gift of healing. In other words, under that particular circumstance, the "best" gift would be the gift of healing, not the word of wisdom. In that sense, the best gift would really be the one that is

needed at the time. Praise God! Paul said, *"But covet earnestly the best gifts..."* (1 Cor. 12:31). The dictionary defines "covet", as to desire earnestly. In other words, Paul urges us to desire earnestly spiritual gifts. Many people have desires, but they are not very earnest about making sure those desires are fulfilled. But let us desire the manifestation of

spiritual gifts among us. Let us covet them as a body of believers, as a group, and let us pray for them to be manifested in our midst. It is all right to pray that the mighty Holy Ghost will manifest Himself among

us dividing to every man severally as He wills according to the scripture (1 Cor. 12:11).

Let me encourage you as a believer to start praying for the fullness of the spiritual gifts to be in manifestation. That is not a prayer to be prayed once and then abandoned. We pray until we see it fully manifested for the benefit of the body of Christ. Those manifesting them must not use

them for monetary gains and be full of pride. They are gifts of grace and must be handled cautiously. You can desire and demand them through prayers for your profiting and that of the body of Christ.

Chapter 9

The Fruits Of The Spirit

The other amazing blessing that comes when we receive the Holy Spirit is the ability to bear fruit. The nine-fold manifestations of the fruits of
the born-again human spirit are a result of the Holy Spirit's indwelling presence. Whilst the gifts of the spirit are for power, the fruits of the spirit are also for character. Godly character is imparted into your spirit that makes you unique and different from those who do not have the Holy Spirit. Bearing these fruits is what qualifies you for heaven after
salvation. Paul listed them in Galatians 5:22-23 *"But the fruit of the Spirit is love, joy, peace, longsuffering, gentleness, goodness, faith, meekness, temperance: against such there is no law."*

These fruits make you unbeatable in the race of life; you display love instead of hatred, joy instead of sadness, peace instead of anxiety, longsuffering instead of anger, gentleness instead of fighting, goodness
instead of wickedness, faith instead of fear, meekness instead of pride and temperance instead of impatience. As we yield to God and obey His Word, the life of the Holy Spirit within us causes us to grow continually in love, joy and peace, as well as the other fruits of the spirit. We can see that one of the main purposes of the indwelling presence of the Holy Spirit in the life of the believer is fruit bearing. Your ability to manifest these fruits makes you a person ready for the second coming of Christ. Your life also becomes a testimony and a challenge to unbelievers. You live above the world with these fruits coming from you.

Chapter 10

The Anointing

The Holy Spirit is the anointing. We can say the anointing is the burden removing, yoke-destroying power of God.
Isaiah 10:27, "And it shall come to pass in that day, that his burden shall be taken away from off thy shoulder, and his yoke from off thy neck, and the yoke shall be destroyed because of the anointing." The anointing is simply the power of God. John G. Lake compared the anointing to electricity. He said "electricity is God's power in the natural realm, but the Holy Ghost power is God's power in the spirit realm" Jesus spoke about the anointing in (Luke 4:18-19) *"The Spirit of the Lord is upon me, because he hath anointed me to preach the gospel to the poor;*

he hath sent me to heal the brokenhearted, to preach deliverance to the captives, and recovering of sight to the blind, to set at liberty them that are bruised, To preach the acceptable year of the Lord."

The word 'anointing' is both a verb and a noun. Anointing can mean the substance used to anoint a person; the anointing oil. In the same vein, the anointing can also mean the act of pouring oil on someone. Understand what it means to be anointed: the word 'anoint' comes from the Hebrew word 'Mashach' meaning to 'rub' or 'smear' with oil. It depicts the presence of God that rubs on a person like oil, meaning His presence remains on you causing the release of power that changes people, situations and things.

So we see that the anointing is the power that changes bad into good and curses into blessings. The anointing blesses you so much that anything that comes into contact with you is blessed; that is, it is empowered to do well or prosper. It is a supernatural ability from the Holy Spirit that empowers us to heal, teach, preach and restore.

HOLY SPIRIT MY PARTNER FOR ALL ROUND SUCCESS

The anointing also refers to the person (power) of the Holy Spirit given to you to perform a given task or assignment or mission. So therefore an anointed person is someone who is inundated (covered) with the anointing of the Holy Spirit. Peter talking about Jesus in the house of Cornelius said; *"How God anointed Jesus of Nazareth with the Holy Ghost and with power: who went about doing good, and healing all that were oppressed of the devil; for God was with him." (Acts 10:38)*

All the great things that happened in Jesus' ministry were because of the anointing. It is God's power that rests upon a man and causes him to do extraordinary and impossible things. In the Old Testament, three types of people were anointed; kings, priests and prophets. David occupied all these offices and so we see him talking about the anointing most of the time. He knew more about the anointing of the Holy Spirit.

"But my horn shalt thou exalt like the horn of an unicorn: I shall be anointed with fresh oil." (Psalms 92:10)

David is revealing to us that all the victories recorded during the glorious years of his reign in Israel was as a result of the anointing. He never lost one battle; he was always a success. That must be the story of all anointed people. May you be anointed for success today as you read this book!

When a man is anointed by the Holy Spirit, the anointing will be with him (John 14:17). The anointing will also be upon him (Luke 4:18) and the anointing will be in him (1 John 2:27). This makes the anointed person special because the anointing is God's special power. The anointing of the anointed person is supposed to be a blessing to

humanity as a whole. It is supposed to bring healing, provision, deliverance, joy and restoration to people (Isaiah 61:1-7). However, the anointed must be treated with respect and must be handled
with care. Do not mock the anointed or the anointing. When you mock, despise, disrespect, mishandle and fight the anointed, you are fighting
God. In the days of Elisha, forty-two (42) children met their untimely death when they chose to mock the anointed prophet (2 Kings 2:23-24).

In the days of the Apostles, Ananias and Sapphira also lied to Peter and died instantly because Peter was very anointed. Peter said by lying to
him, they had lied to the Holy Spirit (Acts 5:3-5). We also see Elymas the sorcerer becoming blind instantly when Paul set his eyes upon him.

He tried to resist the gospel Paul and Barnabas were preaching (Acts 13:6-11). We are all being admonished to deal respectfully and cautiously
with the anointed one and his anointing.

It is interesting that the word "Christ", is the Greek translation of the Hebrew word 'messiah' which means ``the anointed one and his
anointing". So when we are dealing with the anointing, we are actually dealing with Christ. No one can fight Christ; so be cautious!

She Insulted Me & ⬧e Church

Sometime ago, we were worshipping in a rented hall when the authorities stood against me and the church. At a meeting to settle our differences, one woman on the other side stood up openly against the church. She rained abuses on the church and insulted me publicly. I was not present at the meeting that day so one of my leaders told her, "please be careful of the man against whom you are raising your voice". She did not listen and continued attacking us till the meeting was over. Few days
later she came down with a stroke and was totally paralyzed. She never recovered from that stroke and passed away a few months later. Attacking the anointed can be deadly so let us watch out! Seek to be

HOLY SPIRIT MY PARTNER FOR ALL ROUND SUCCESS

anointed so you can have all round success because the anointing makes success possible in all things.

EFFECTS OF THE ANOINTING

When you receive the anointing of the Holy Spirit, you are energized from inside to do greater things. *"I can do all things through Christ which strengtheneth me." (Philippians 4:13)*

The "Christ" being referred to in this scripture is not the man Jesus. "Christ" here refers specifically to the anointed one and His anointing.

What Paul was trying to say was that 'He can do all things through the anointed one and His anointing'. In other words, the anointing of the Holy Spirit in me makes me anointed, I can do all things; the hard, the impossible and the unimaginable. Hallelujah! This is the effect of the anointing! David taught us so much about the effects of the anointing.

We will look at a few of them;

- **The anointing distinguishes you and sets you apart for favour** (makes you attractive, charming, and gives you a special aura).

"Thou lovest righteousness, and hatest wickedness: therefore God, thy God, hath anointed thee with the oil of gladness above thy fellows." (Psalms 45:7)

- **The anointing destroys your burdens and yokes.** It takes care of your problems.

"And it shall come to pass in that day, that his burden shall be taken away from off thy shoulder, and his yoke from off thy neck, and the yoke shall be destroyed because of the anointing." (Isaiah 10:27)

- **The anointing crushes and silences your enemies.**

"But my horn shalt thou exalt like the horn of an unicorn: I shall be anointed with fresh oil. Mine eye also shall see my desire on mine enemies, and mine ears shall hear my desire of the wicked that rise up against me. (Psalms 92:10-11)

- **The anointing makes you to flourish, blossom and spread.**

"The righteous shall flourish like the palm tree: he shall grow like a cedar in Lebanon. Those that be planted in the house of the Lord shall flourish in the courts of our God." (Psalms 92:12-13)

- **The anointing makes you fruitful even in old age.** It keeps you young.

"They shall still bring forth fruit in old age; they shall be fat and flourishing;" (Psalms 92:14)

- **The anointing establishes and strengthens you.**

"I have found David my servant; with my holy oil have I anointed him: With whom my hand shall be established: mine arm also shall strengthen him." (Psalms 89:20-21)

Saul was anointed by the Prophet Samuel in 1 Samuel 10:1-7. Let us see the effects of this anointing on Saul after he was anointed.

- **The anointing brings you into captainship** (leadership, it positions you ahead).

"Then Samuel took a vial of oil, and poured it upon his head, and kissed him, and said, Is it not because the Lord hath anointed thee to be captain over his inheritance?" (1 Samuel 10:1)

- **The anointing brings restoration.**

"When thou art departed from me today, then thou shalt find two men by Rachel's sepulchre in the border of Benjamin at Zelzah; and they will say unto thee, the asses which thou wentest to seek are found: ..."
(1 Samuel 10:2)

- **The anointing moves you forward (progress).**

"Then shalt thou go on forward from thence, and thou shalt come to the plain of Tabor, and there shall meet thee three men going up to God to Bethel, one carrying three kids, and another carrying three loaves of bread, and another carrying a bottle of wine:" (1 Samuel 10:3)

- **The anointing will cause people to honour you with gifts** (that is prosperity).

"And they will salute thee, and give thee two loaves of bread; which thou shalt receive of their hands." (1 Samuel 10:4)

HOLY SPIRIT MY PARTNER FOR ALL ROUND SUCCESS

- **The anointing will change your status in life** (a new spiritual office and chair). *"After that thou shalt come to the hill of God, where is the garrison of the Philistines: and it shall come to pass, when thou art come thither to*
the city, that thou shalt meet a company of prophets coming down from the high place with a psaltery, and a tabret, and a pipe, and a harp, before them; and they shall prophesy:" (1 Samuel 10:5)

- **The anointing changes you completely** (you become another man, someone set apart for God).
"And the Spirit of the Lord will come upon thee, and thou shalt prophesy with them, and shalt be turned into another man."
(1 Samuel 10:6)

These are the effects of the anointing. It brings a lot of blessing and honour to a man. Jesus became famous because of the anointing and multitudes followed him everywhere (Luke 4:14). The Apostles turned Jerusalem upside down with miracles, signs and wonders, including
raising the dead (Acts 5:12-16). There is no doubt that the anointing changes lives. Everyone who was anointed influenced his world because
of the powerful effects of the anointing. We all must desire the anointing in greater measure because the anointing is in levels. May you be
anointed as you go through the pages of this book!

Chapter 11

How To Catch The Anointing

Now that we have seen how powerful the anointing of the Holy Ghost is, we must find out how to catch the anointing. The anointing, because
it is valuable comes at a cost. It is free but not cheap. In scripture we saw Elisha following Elijah for many years. Finally he asked for a double portion of his anointing and Elijah told him, *"You have asked for a hard thing, nevertheless if you see me going, you will have it (2 Kings 2:1-14).*

Catching the anointing begins with a strong desire for the anointing.

How Do You Catch The Anointing?

- **You must be thirsty for the anointing.**

Isaiah 44:3 says, "For I will pour water upon him that is thirsty, and floods upon the dry ground: I will pour my spirit upon thy seed, and my blessing
upon thine offspring:"

- **You must serve for the anointing.**

You are likely to catch any anointing you serve under. When you serve the anointed with an open heart, you will receive a transfer of the anointing. Elisha is referred to as one that pours water on Elijah. That means he was Elijah's servant.

"But Jehoshaphat said, Is there not here a prophet of the Lord, that we may enquire of the Lord by him? And one of the king of Israel's servants answered and said, Here is Elisha the son of Shaphat, which poured water on the hands of Elijah." (2 Kings 3:11)

- **Receive the anointed as a father.**

This is because inheritance flows from fathers to children. Humble yourself and receive the carrier of the particular anointing that you
desire as a father. Honour him as a father in your heart. Elisha called Elijah 'My father', my father (2 Kings 2:12).

- **Follow the anointed for a long time and something will rub on you.**

Elisha followed Elijah from Gilgah to Bethel, Bethel to Jericho and Jericho to Jordan (2 Kings 2-6). They travelled together for sometime before he caught the double portion anointing. Other ways of following is through books, CDs and DVDs. Reading the anointed books and hearing the anointed voices of anointed men of God will make you anointed. "And the spirit entered into me when he spake unto me, and set me upon my feet, that I heard him that spake unto me." (Ezekiel 2:2)

Let us examine how great men of God received the anointing on other men by interacting with them and their materials

- **Reading anointed books**

Papa Hagin (Rev Kenneth Hagin) of blessed memory once said "I read almost everything that Smith Wigglesworth ever wrote, actually wearing his books out until something from him rubbed off on me." He was saying that the anointing on Wigglesworth (the great Apostle of faith who raised 23 people from the dead) was transferred to him as he kept reading his materials.

- **Listening to anointed teachings**

Bishop David Oyedepo one time attended a conference held in Tulsa Oklahoma by Papa Hagin. According to his testimony, in one of the afternoon sessions, Papa Hagin was ministering and he positioned himself for an encounter even though he sat far way in the gallery. He was sensitive and listening attentively when suddenly he saw the face of the man of God transfigured like that of a little baby with oil dripping down his cheeks. As he kept watching him, something was fired into him from the man of God. He began to cry uncontrollably like a baby.

He then heard a voice saying "My son David, the baton has been passed on to you". Today the anointing of the word of faith which Papa Hagin spear-headed visibly rests upon him. He has done amazing things by faith like the building of a 50,000-seater auditorium in one year, debt

free in 1999- reputed to be the largest church auditorium in the world). Transfer of the anointing is real.

- **Watching anointed videos**

Bishop David Oyedepo also received the anointing for performing miracles by watching a video of a miracle crusade by Archbishop Benson Idahosa in 1987. He said "My heart and eyes were glued to the programme. While watching and listening to the crusade message, the

power of God impacted me so strongly that I found myself in tears, there alone in my house! I went to bed in that state and there was a quickening

in me. I rose up early, went to my living room and cried out, "God show me the secret!" And in the midst of this experience, I heard a man walk

in and put his hands on my back and some waves went through my spine. I exploded in tears. The following day which was Sunday, he stood

up in church to welcome the people. As soon as he read Psalm 110, the power of God broke out and all kinds of miracles and healings took

place. The anointing of miracles was caught from watching a video tape. You can also catch it after the same order. Refuse to be dry in the

ministry. You must be anointed.

- **Listening to anointed messages on audio devices**

Bishop Dag Heward Mills also received the transfer of anointing while

he was listening to a preaching tape by Kenneth Hagin. Something was

fired into him and he heard these words" Now you can teach". Today he is one of the greatest teachers in the ministry with vibrant churches all

over the world. The anointing is transferable and you can attract any anointing on a man of God if only you follow the steps that are being

taught. I see you becoming anointed as you are reading this book.

- **Laying on of hands**

The power of God is transferable. When an anointed man lays his hands on you, he can transfer the anointing to you. The anointing can flow like water.

"And Joshua the son of Nun was full of the spirit of wisdom; for Moses had laid his hands upon him: and the children of Israel hearkened unto him, and did as the Lord commanded Moses." (Deuteronomy 34:9)

Timothy also received a transfer of the spirit by the laying on of Hands

"Wherefore I put thee in remembrance that thou stir up the gift of God, which is in thee by the putting on of my hands." (2 Timothy 1:6)

- **Honoring the anointed with seeds**

When you honour a man of God with a gift; money or any precious material object, it can trigger the release of the anointing. Jacob got his father's blessing after giving his father the best food he desired (Gen 27:1-29). Personally I have received anointings and different graces from honoring men of God with financial seeds. Every year, I make sure I honour my spiritual fathers and mentors with seeds. I also follow them as closely as possible through books, CDs and DVDs. I am walking in some anointing as a result of that. Praise God! You are next in line to be anointed.

- **Catching the anointing through prayers and fasting**

You must be praying and fasting for anything you desire. You must suppress your flesh and give the spirit the upper hand to take over. Jesus said' This kind can come forth by nothing, but by prayer and fasting (Mark 9:29). He was saying that you cannot carry a high degree of power except you pay the price of prayer and fasting. He personally showed us

HOLY SPIRIT MY PARTNER FOR ALL ROUND SUCCESS

an example in Luke 4:1,14 & 18. He went into the wilderness to pray and fast. He returned in the power of the Holy Spirit (v14), and the anointing
to preach, heal and restore came upon him (v18).
Everyone who desires the anointing must pray for long hours and fast alongside. Anyone walking in the anointing is a success. I see you becoming the next anointed person in town in the name of Jesus!

Chapter 12

How To Activate The Power of The Holy Spirit

After the first experience which is the baptism of the Holy Ghost with the evidence of speaking in tongues (Acts 2:4), you must continue to be

filled every now and then. We must walk in the overflow of the spirit (Acts 4:31). We are told to stir the spirit (the gift of God) in us.

"Wherefore I put thee in remembrance that thou stir up the gift of God, which is in thee by the putting on of my hands." 2 Timothy 1:6

To stir up the Spirit you must:

- **Be thirsty**

You must have a strong desire for the fellowship of the Holy Spirit.

"For I will pour water upon him that is thirsty, and floods upon the dry ground: I will pour my spirit upon thy seed, and my blessing upon thine offspring:" (Isaiah 44:3)

- **Walk in the light of His word**

The Holy Ghost wrote the bible so when you practice His word; you are

in agreement with Him (Amos 3:3).

"Knowing this first, that no prophecy of the scripture is of any private interpretation. For the prophecy came not in old time by the will of man: but holy men of God spake as they were moved by the Holy Ghost (2 Peter 1:20-21)

- **Pray in tongues consistently**

"For if I pray in an unknown tongue, my spirit prayeth, but my understanding is unfruitful." (1 Corinthians 14:14)

In Jude 1:20, you build yourself up by praying in the Holy Ghost. That is the source of all the signs and wonders and miracles! All of these signs and wonders are in the Holy Spirit and He is in us. Prayer, then, is going to play the major role in this outpouring. Prayer, based on the word, is the doorway into the mightiest release of

power known to man. It brings the presence of God to and upon men in any part of the world. That power operates as believers pray in faith,

allowing those rivers of living water to gush toward the dry and thirsty.

- **Worship and praise God in the Spirit**

We mingle our human spirit with the Holy Spirit as we sing spiritual songs in worship and praise of Him.

"And be not drunk with wine, wherein is excess; but be filled with the Spirit; Speaking to yourselves in psalms and hymns and spiritual songs, singing and making melody in your heart to the Lord; Giving thanks always for all things unto God and the Father in the name of our Lord Jesus Christ;"

(Ephesians 5:18-20)

We get filled with His power to the overflow. We are inundated with His presence that gives us all round (total) success in all we do, because we

do them through the Holy Spirit.

- **Walk in love**

We maintain our daily fellowship with the Holy Spirit by walking in the love of God and showing love towards our neighbours. We live life

devoid of hatred, unforgiveness and bitterness, these will impede the anointing.

"And hope maketh not ashamed; because the love of God is shed abroad in our hearts by the Holy Ghost which is given unto us."

(Romans 5:5)

Anyone who wants to be anointed and walk in the overflow must walk in love.

LESSONS FROM DR. KENNETH COPELAND

HOLY SPIRIT MY PARTNER FOR ALL ROUND SUCCESS

This is what Jerry Savelle learned from Dr. Kenneth Copeland concerning the anointing of the Holy Ghost and how to prepare for a meeting (from his book, *"IN THE FOOTSTEPS OF A PROPHET – Jerry Savelle*).

"One of the things you need to learn about the anointing is if you want it to operate strongly in your life, then discipline yourself to spend much

time with God before every service. Don't run around with people before service, and then run into the Church, get behind the pulpit, and expect

the anointing to be strong. The anointing flows out of your innermost being. It is like rivers of water in the very core of your spirit. Protect it,

and it will be there when you need it.

You cannot give someone something that you don't have. You cannot expect to transfer anointing to someone if you have not prepared

yourself properly to operate in the anointing. If you do not have it, you certainly cannot give it to someone else. This is the reason it is so

important that you never allow anyone or anything to rob you of your prayer time before a meeting.

This is what Brother Oral Roberts taught Brother Copeland. He knew that after 3:00 in the afternoon, you could not talk to Oral Roberts.

Neither could you talk to me after 3pm in the afternoon when I am in a meeting. I lock myself away and prepare for that meeting and I do not

engage in conversation with others. I could see the results in Brother Copeland's life, and that is what I wanted. A lot of people see results, but

they are not willing to do what it takes to go to them.

Brother Copeland went on to say: this is the reason that it is so important that you do not allow anyone or anything to rob you of your prayer time. Get alone with God. He is the only One who can do anything for the people to whom you are ministering. If you get alone with God, then His anointing will come on you, and then you will have something to transmit into the people. Without the anointing, you have nothing to offer them. Everyone wants to be anointed, but few people know how to get in position to receive. To get in position to receive that anointing, you must fellowship with God. Sometimes, it is a lonely life. Sometimes, you feel like you are the loneliest person in the world when you are shut away. But when you come out, and you operate in that anointing, you feel like the most blessed person in the world because God has used you to bring deliverance to others. In order to become strong in the anointing, you must become single-minded. Your primary purpose in ministry: meet the needs of the people. Bring deliverance everywhere you go." I would want to urge everyone working for God in any area or department to spend time in prayer and fellowship with the Lord to stir up the anointing before you minister. Be it a chorister, preacher, usher, choreographer etc. We must all learn from the lessons shared by Jerry Savelle from Dr. Copeland. You shall be anointed from this day forward! As you read this book and walk in the light of these revelations, I see you becoming the closest partner of the Holy Spirit, full of power that guarantees all round success! God bless you!

AMAZING TESTIMONIES

These testimonies as well as many others you find in Christianity are engineered by the Holy Spirit - The grand commander of signs and wonders. As you read them, may the Holy Spirit duplicate them in your own life in Jesus name!

Tumour Melts Miraculously

When I first came to the church, I prayed to God, telling Him that I do not want to tell my problem to the man of God, so if He truly wants me to stay in the church, He should let the man of God locate me. On the 24th of April

this year (2016), Daddy called for people who were booked for an operation to walk to the altar and I joined. I had a tumor in my stomach and I had

been booked for an operation, but I never went; I believed God for divine healing.

After Daddy prayed for us that Sunday, I woke up the next day seeing clots of blood coming out of me and I was not menstruating. I just knew then,

that it was the power of God, melting the tumor away. God has set me free without surgery. I thank God for the life of the man of God.- **Awuradjoa**

Saved from death

I am a twin and in the same senior high school with my sister. Three days before we started WASSCE, my sister and I prepared to go to class to study throughout the night at around 11:00pm. Just before we stepped out of the

dormitory, my sister started complaining of stomach pains. My friend and I rushed her to the hospital immediately and she was admitted. The nurses then put a drip on her. After about 3 minutes, her breath ceased and she became very stiff and cold. My sister had died. The nurses then took the drip off her and called the doctor. The doctor came to the ward and

instructed the nurses to put the drip back on her but they could not locate her veins to insert the syringe. My friend and I then rushed to the dormitory and picked the bottle of anointing oil Daddy gave us before we left for school. We went back to the entrance of the hospital, poured some
of the oil in our hands and declared that, if Rev. Dr. Kwadwo Boateng Bempah be a man of God, God should revive my sister. We then began praying. By then, my sister had died for about three hours. A few minutes after we began praying, a nurse came out to call us because my sister had
come back to life and the stomach pain had ceased as well. She was discharged that same day and was told to come back the next day for a laboratory check-up.

After several tests were conducted, they found no sickness. I thank God for the life of Daddy and for saving my sister from death. **-Alberta**

24 Hour Financial Breakthrough

I was invited for the last 14 days prayer and fasting in April and during one Thursday evening session, Bishop instructed us to write down a miracle we were expecting in the next 24hours and put it on the floor and declared over it. I obeyed and wrote GHS 2000.00($526) as the amount I needed and believed it. I got to work the next day and in less than the 24 hours declared, I received a text message on my phone from my work place that GHS 2,700 ($710)
has been deposited into my account which is amazing. I thank God for this miracle. - **Iris**

Supernatural debt Cancellation

My mom had borrowed money from 3 different banks because of a project, totalling GHC 15,000 ($3,947). Since then, things got tough, as she was trying to pay back the money. During the career and business breakthrough
service in March, I brought all the bank documents as my point of contact because as a student, I did not know how my mother was going to pay my fees for the next semester because of the situation. During the service,

HOLY SPIRIT MY PARTNER FOR ALL ROUND SUCCESS

Bishop declared prophetically that debts would be cancelled and I believed it. I called my mother after the service to tell her that, her debt will be cancelled. Five days later, she had a call from the first bank, and they told her she had finished paying her debt. Within the next hour, another call came from her workplace, congratulating her for the payment of her debt.

She said for a moment, she thought she was being mocked. Finally, the last bank also called her and said, "Madam, you have finished paying your loan and you even have an extra GHC1,200 ($316) in your account". I thank God for this awesome miracle. **- Jackie**

Divine Healing from Hypertension

For the past 8 years, I had been suffering from very high blood pressure, which could rise to 200mmHg and this was very alarming because I could easily suffer a stroke. I was therefore to be on drugs always, even though they could only reduce my blood pressure to 150mmHg. I came for service one day and Daddy called for those with an incurable disease to come to the altar and I did. After we had been prayed for, I decided not to take the drugs anymore till my next checkup. To God be the glory, my pressure had decreased to 56mmHg! **- K. Atta**

You are next in line for a Holy Ghost miracle! Congratulations for reading this powerful book. You have just received fresh anointing. Make these powerful declarations now:

I am a successful Christian.

I cannot fail.

I have a life of endless possibilities because I am in partnership with the Holy Spirit.

JESUS IS LORD.

Don't miss out!

Visit the website below and you can sign up to receive emails whenever Kwadwo Boateng Bempah publishes a new book. There's no charge and no obligation.

https://books2read.com/r/B-A-JEXWC-XCQJF

BOOKS2READ

Connecting independent readers to independent writers.

Also by Kwadwo Boateng Bempah

Engaging The Law Of Seedtime And Harvest for Abundant Overflow
God of Miracles
Holy Spirit My Partner for All Round Success
Jesus The Great Physician: He is the master surgeon who heals all manner of sicknesses and diseases